This book is based on a true story of a young boy's experience as the shepherd to the neighbor's sheep. It's a depiction of Jesus the Good Shepherd from the gospel of John 10.

Dedicated to those that strive and value the necessity of teaching biblical truths to the next generation.

Email address: kdoer2011@aol.com

His Sheep Hear His Voice

Kathy Doerscher   Illustrated by Susan Thompson

My name is Lonnie and I remember the day when the sheep on a neighbor's farm helped me to understand why Jesus spoke in parables.

A parable is like a riddle or a story. Jesus used a parable when he said he is the Good Shepherd and his sheep hear his voice.

While working at the neighbor's farm, my older brother Bubba Ray and I were told to prepare the pool and give the sheep a bath. My other brother Arthur went to work in the field.

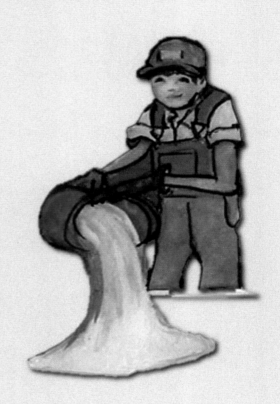

We called the sheep from the barn, but they would not listen. No matter how loud we called, they would not listen.

Then my brother Arthur came to help us.

He called to the sheep and they followed him out of the barn and jumped right in the pool.

When Bubba and I saw this, our jaws dropped to the floor in amazement. Seeing our shocked faces, Arthur said, "I came back to help you when I realized you were going to have a problem getting the sheep to listen to you."

Arthur went on to explain,
"I had to spend a lot of
time with the sheep before
they would listen to me.

A few months ago, one of
the sheep kept getting lost
when he wandered off from
the other sheep. He would
scream for hours. It took a
while before he was willing
to trust me and follow me."

"Now, whenever I find him lost, I just call him, 'Wanderer, come on' and he knows my voice and follows me back to the other sheep.

I guess I've become the sheep's shepherd. This has helped me to understand why Jesus said he is our Good Shepherd."

Bubba and I were confused,
I said "What? I don't understand.
Jesus is our Good Shepherd? But
people aren't sheep."
Arthur explained, "Jesus often
spoke in parables to get our
attention.
Your jaw didn't really hit the floor,
but the words drew a picture we
could see in our mind. Parables can
do the same thing. They help us
to understand heavenly things
that we cannot see."

Still confused, I asked, "But why would Jesus use sheep to get our attention?"

Arthur answered, "Lonnie, that's because sheep learn to hear and respond only to the voice of their trusted shepherd. Therefore, a thief cannot trick the sheep into following him instead. Jesus wants us to hear and know his voice, and to trust him. When we only follow his voice, we will not be tricked into following the Thief."

Arthur continued, "These sheep learned to hear and respond only to my voice. At night, I put the sheep in the barn to protect them from danger. Then in the morning, they get all excited when they hear my voice call their name, 'Come on Wanderer.' 'Good morning Wooly.' 'You're looking marvelous today Snowball...'".

"Just like when mom comes to pick you up from school. Not everyone gets excited to hear the sound of her voice. Nor are they willing to follow her voice out of the classroom. Sheep are similar, except they don't even respond unless they hear their shepherd's voice."

"Jesus said 'I am the door; if anyone enters through me, he will be saved, and will go in and out and find pasture.'"

"As our Good Shepherd, Jesus told us 'the thief comes only to steal and kill and destroy; I came that they may have life, and have it abundantly.'"

"In biblical times, the owner of the sheep would often pay someone else to care for the sheep. When a wolf would come, the paid man would often run away in fear, with no concern for the sheep.

Jesus is not a paid shepherd, he is the Good Shepherd, who gave his life for us."

Arthur continued, "Jesus provides his sheep with green pastures."
Bubba Ray responded, "But people don't eat grass."

Arthur explained, "Remember, it's a parable. Just like sheep need grass to grow strong physically, we need to feast on God's Word to grow strong spiritually."

This lesson helped me to understand why Jesus often spoke in parables, using examples to help us to understand heavenly things that we cannot see.

I learned how important it is for us to feast on God's Word. Like sheep, we can know and follow the voice of Jesus our Good Shepherd and not get tricked into following the Thief.

Made in the USA
Middletown, DE
30 June 2020